TABLE OF CONTE

GW01191847

About the Author

Kelly Weeks is a talented, young and energetic musician who began his musical career as a singer/songwriter, playing solo and with bands in the Minneapolis, Boston and Orlando areas. After completing his Bachelor's degree in Professional Music from the Berklee College of Music, Kelly went on to provide private lessons to students of all ages in his home town of Minneapolis in 2003. In order to further his teaching and musical abilities, Kelly completed a K-12 Instrumental Teaching License from Hamline University and completed his Master's degree in Instrumental Education in 2012

Kelly has extensive experience teaching students of varying levels and needs in both the public school system and in private settings. In addition, Kelly is an accomplished songwriter, whose songs can currently be heard on various MTV shows as well as The Young and the Restless.

How to Use This Book

This is a beginner guitar method for kids. It consists of 25 play-along songs that teach basic playing techniques. It is intended to show you how to play along with music recordings. This book doesn't focus on one style or technique. Instead it gives an introduction to several different techniques used to play the guitar. The purpose of this is to give the student an opportunity to become successful in at least one area of the guitar. This book is meant to make learning the guitar a fun process. It isn't a comprehensive method. It is simply a method to engage students by having them play along with fun songs on their guitar. It is strongly recommended to use this book with private music lessons. There is no replacement for the instant feedback of a professional teacher.

Technique

The three main techniques that will be taught in this book are picking, finger picking and strumming. The specific technique will change from song to song. These techniques will be described in the song descriptions when you learn them. Please assume that you will use a guitar pick to play each song unless you are instructed otherwise.

TUNING

This book uses standard tuning. This means that your guitar strings should be tuned like this.

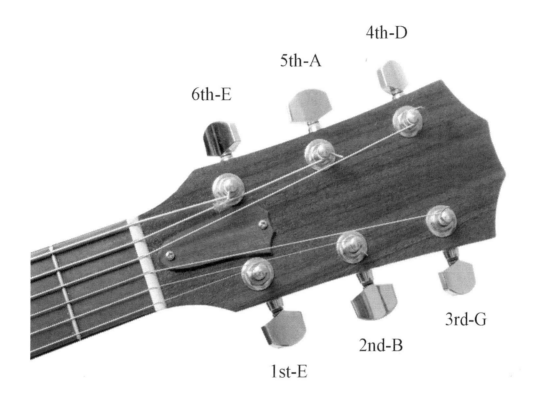

4th-D
5th-A
6th-E
3rd-G
2nd-B
1st-E

To remember this sequence say "Eddie-Ate-Dynamite-Good-Bye-Eddie." The best way to tune your guitar is with an electronic tuner. You should invest some money in an electronic tuner. It will make tuning much easier for you.

TABLATURE

Tablature is the written form of notation that is widely used for the guitar. In a nutshell, tablature indicates the location of a note on the fret board. Tablature shows six lines which represent the six strings on the guitar. The top line represents the first string, which is the string on the guitar that is closest to the floor as you hold it, also known as the high E string. The bottom line represents the sixth string, which is the thickest string in diameter. The 4/4 at the beginning of the song is called a time signature. This indicates that in each measure there are four beats and that a quarter is what is used to count the beat. The two dots at the end of this tablature example tell you to repeat back to the beginning and play the song again.

Each song includes the standard notation above the tablature. Since this book is not a comprehensive method, not much explanation will be given to the standard notation. Most of the directions will refer to the tablature instead. The standard notation is there for your convenience. It is not required of you to know how to read it to play the songs in this book. Use the notation if you can. There are many good books available for learning to read music notation on the guitar.

PLAYING POSITION

The position in which the guitar is held while playing is very important and deserves attention.

Standing Position
If you practice standing up it is strongly recommended that you use a shoulder strap to keep the guitar in the correct position. The height at which the guitar hangs from your shoulder should position the guitar at about belly button level or a little higher. It should hang down in front of your body and be closer to side of your strumming hand. The angle of the guitar should position the tuners higher than the body of the guitar. The neck of the guitar should not be parallel with the ground.

Seated Position
The strap is not as important as in the standing position but it is still highly recommended. If you are right handed then the guitar should sit on your right thigh. The guitar should balance on your thigh so that it is not supported by your left hand. Position the guitar so that it angles the head stock up slightly. The guitar shoud be held secure under your strumming hand arm. If a strap is used in the seated position it should position the guitar in the same way as it was in the standing position.

AUDIO AND VIDEO RECORDINGS

Each song is accompanied with an audio recording and/or video. Use these recordings to look, listen and learn the rhythms for each song. If you have not learned a counting method for rhythms then these recordings will be very important to your learning. As you play each song keep referring back to the recordings to make sure that you are playing the songs correctly. To hear or watch the songs please logon to http://kellysmusicbooks.com/media. Some digital versions should have the media built in.

PARTS

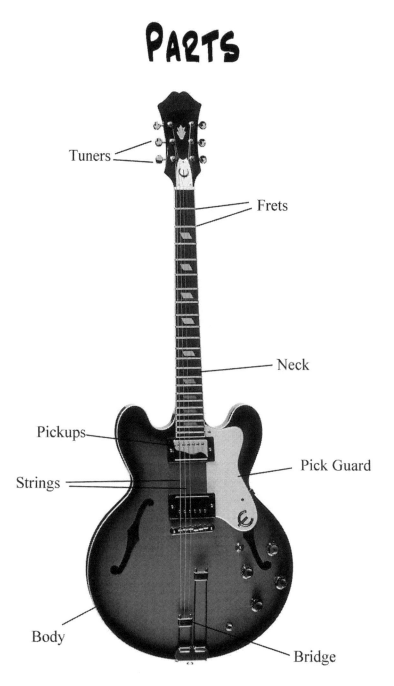

Tuners

Frets

Neck

Pickups

Pick Guard

Strings

Body

Bridge

CHORD DIAGRAMS

Chord diagrams are a snapshot of the first five frets of the guitar. The Cmaj7 at the top tells you the name of the chord. The thick, black horizontal line represents the nut of the guitar. The rest of the horizontal lines represent the frets. The vertical lines are the strings of the guitar which are numbered from right to left, 1, 2, 3, 4, 5, and 6. The black circles represent the places that you are supposed to press with your fingers. Lastly, the circles above the nut indicate that these strings should be played open and x's mean that the string should be avoided or muted. When you play Cmaj7 you need to use two fingers of your fretting hand. The first note is on the third fret 5th string and the other note is on the second fret 4th string.

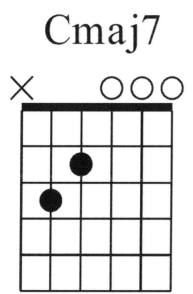

1. 2 NOTE JAM

This song will teach you to pick two different notes. You will need a guitar pick to play this song and most of the songs in this book. Hold the guitar pick between your thumb and pointer finger. Pick with a downward motion.

Both of the notes are on the 6th string, which is the thickest string. First pick the 6th string open three times. To play a string "open" means that you don't press down on the string with your fretting hand. Now, press down on the 5th fret and play the string three more times. To find the fifth fret first put the pointer finger of your fretting on the plastic part (nut) at the end of the neck by the head stock. Then slide your finger so that it's between the nut and the first metal fret. This is the first fret. Count from this fret by sliding your finger over the metal frets toward the body of the guitar until you count up to five. The fifth fret usually has a dot on it.

1

2. SURF'S UP

In this surf rock song you will play four different notes on the 6th string. Use a guitar pick to play all the notes and play with a downward motion. The first note is on the fifth fret. You will then descend to the third fret, then the first fret, and then you will play the string open. Play all the notes two times. Listen to the audio recording and try to play along with the song.

Tips

The two dots at the end of the song mean to repeat back to the beginning. Keep repeating the song until the music stops

3. HIP-HOP-POP

You will now get a chance to play notes on the 5th string. Start by playing the 6th string open three times. Listen to the recording for the correct rhythm. Then play the third fret 6th string. Now, switch to the third fret 5th string and then finally play the 5th string open. You can use either your pointer finger or middle finger to fret the notes.

Tips
If you have a hard time playing with the recordings practice the song several times by yourself and then try playing along again.

4. SURF'S UP-1ST STRING

This is a 1st string rendition of the second song in this book "Surf's Up." The first string is the one that sounds the highest but is closest to the floor in height. It's a little more difficult to play the first string because it's easy to accidently play the wrong string. All the notes in this song are on the first string. First play the fifth fret, then the third, then the first and then the open string.

Tips
After you play each pair of notes quickly silence the string. When you stop the string from ringing it's called a rest. The quarter note rests are represented in the notation with a squiggly vertical line.

5. SCARY RIFF

This song will give you a chance to use different fingers of your fretting hand. The fingers of your fretting hand are numbered: pointer-1, middle-2, ring-3, pinky-4. The finger numbers are written above the tablature in the standard notation. Please check to make sure that you are using the correct fingers for each note. Watch the video to make sure that you are doing it right.

Tips
It is very important to get good at using all of your fingers to play notes. Don't let yourself get into the habit of only using one finger to play songs.

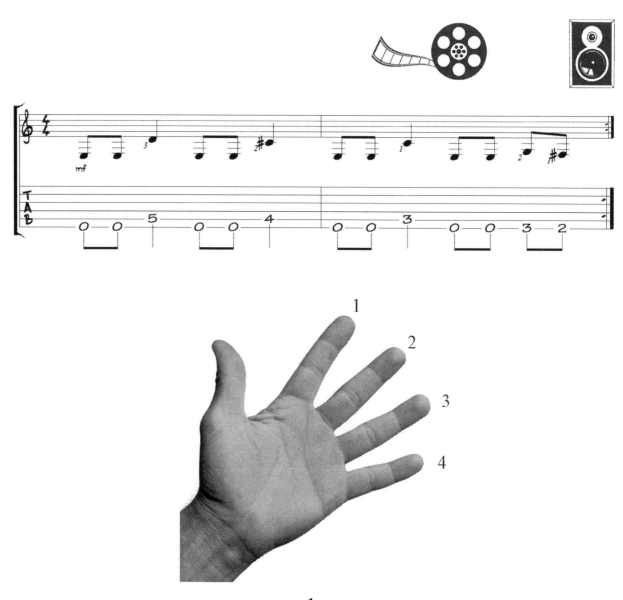

6. ROCK OUT

In this song you will have to rock out and it will require some fast picking. There are four different notes and they are all on the 6th string. First play the fifth fret. The rhythm is counted 1-2-3-e-and-a-4. Next play the eighth fret, then play the twelfth fret and then play the open string. Use the same rhythm throughout the song.

Tips

If you make a mistake keep playing as if you didn't. This is very important as it will prepare you to play with other musicians.

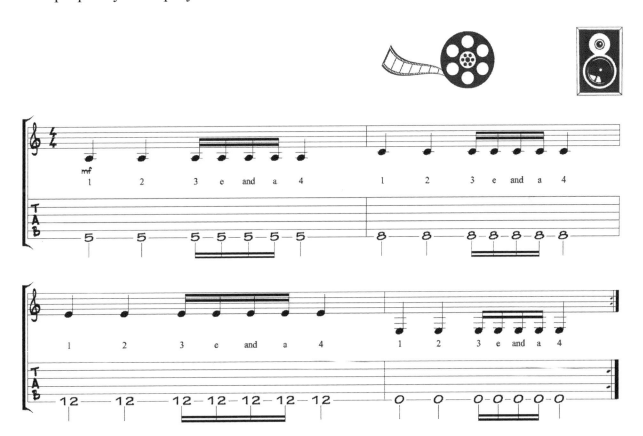

7. MELLOW STRUM

This song introduces the technique of strumming. Strumming means that you are going to use your pick to play more than one string at the same time. Watch the video for guidance. In this song you will be strumming two chords. The chords are G major and C major 7. To play G major put your middle finger on the 6th string third fret, then put your pointer finger on the 5th string second fret. Hold both fingers down and then strum all the strings except the 1st string. Strum this chord four times. To play Cmaj7 simply move both of your fingers down a string from G major. Your middle finger should be on the 5th string third fret and your pointer finger should be on the 4th string second fret. Strum all the strings except the 6th string.

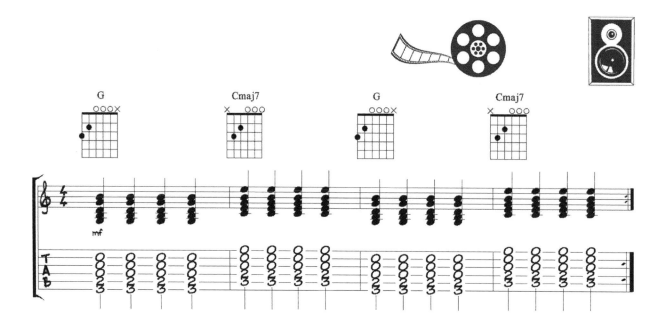

Tips

If you can't remember how to read the chord diagrams above the music then go to the foreward in this book and read the explanation. There are many versions of the same chord. You should learn several ways to play the same chord.

8. LA TUNE

There are seven elements that make up music. One of them is called form. This song features the song form A-B. What this means is that this song is made of two separate repeating parts. Please refer to the tablature for all the notes. The first section is the A section. Play the A section four times. Now, go on to the B section and play it four times. After you have played both sections repeat the entire song one more time.

Tips
The B section is almost identical to the A section. The only difference is that the first two notes are not the same.

9. COUNTRY STRUMMING

Country Strumming will teach you to switch between two very common chords, G major and E minor. This song has a country-twang sound. Strum the E minor three times and then repeat, then switch to the G major chord. Strum G major three times and then repeat. Use your pointer finger and middle finger to play the notes of each chord.

Tips

Keep your pointer finger pressed down for both chords. You don't have to pick it up when you switch. The G major voicing in this song is a simplified version.

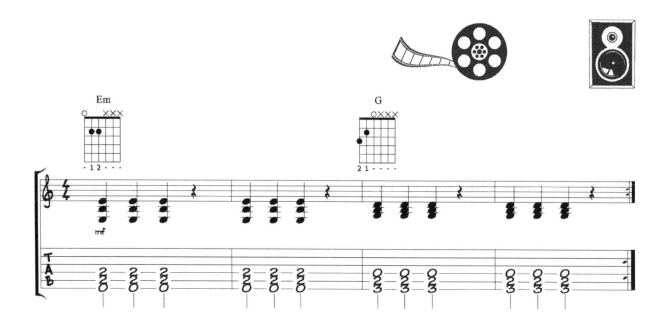

10. RASTA MAN

Reggae music comes from Jamaica. It has a unique groove and an off-beat rhythm. You will strum two string chords in this reggae song. To play the first chord hold both the first and second strings down at the fifth fret. You can use two fingers or you can lay one finger flat over both strings. This technique is called "barring." Barring is a very important technique that you will see often in more advanced songs. Play the second chord the same way only at the seventh fret. Listen carefully to the music to hear the rhythm of the guitar.

Tips

Silence the strings of the guitar between strums for an authentic reggae sound. You can do this with either your strumming hand or fretting finger.

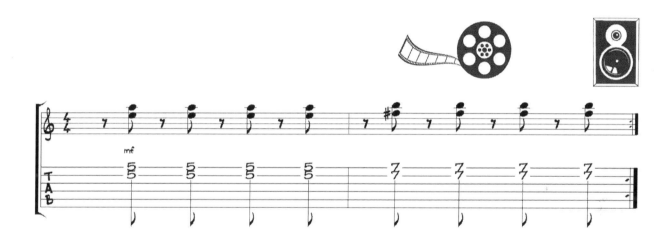

11. POWERFUL CHORDS

Behold the power chord! Power chords are two note chords that are normally played on the 6th, 5th, or 4th strings. When you hear them you will immediately think of rock music. There are three power chords in this song. They are E5, A5, and D5. Strum only the strings indicated in the tablature. Use your pointer finger to play all the second fret notes.

Tips
The picture below the tablature shows where you should put your finger for the first chord of the song.

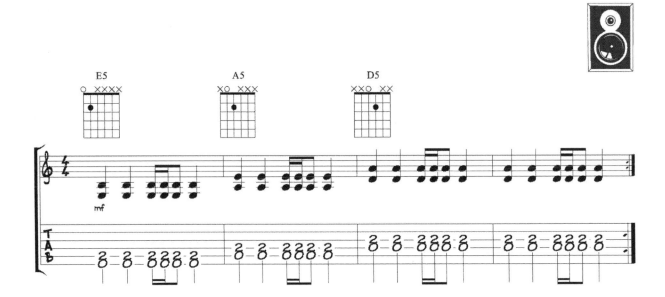

12. A FAMILIAR MELODY

This is a Reggae version of "Twinkle Twinkle Little Star." The entire melody is played on the first string except for the ending. This song is probably familiar to you, which normally makes learning faster. Try to play along with the recording. Playing with the recording is harder but is better practice. It prepares you for playing with other musicians. Pick all notes with a downward motion.

12

13. MY DAD'S FIRST SONG

This is a classic guitar riff that became popular in early rock n' roll and rhythm and blues. Use your 1st finger (pointer) to play the second fret notes and your 3rd finger (ring) to play the fourth fret notes. This riff is basically an extension of the power chords used in the previous song Powerful Chords.

Tips

While you play the fourth fret notes, try to keep your pointer finger held down.

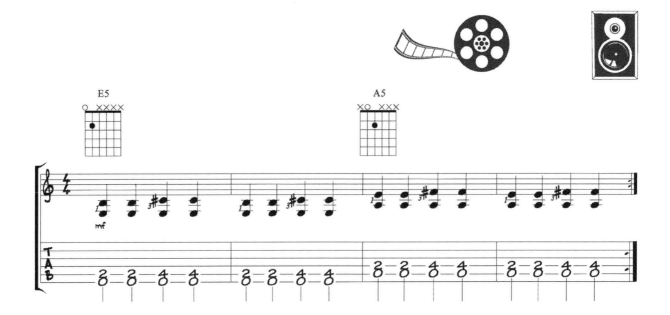

14. FINGER PICKING SONG

This song will teach you a new technique, finger picking. Finger picking is a technique in which you use your fingers instead of a guitar pick to play the strings. To play this song play the 6th string with your thumb, the 2nd string with your pointer finger, the 3rd string with your thumb, and the 1st string with your middle finger. It is a four note pattern. Keep repeating the notes over and over again until you can play them without much effort.

Tips
Since this is a new technique, take your time and allow yourself to make mistakes. Finger picking is a different approach to the guitar.

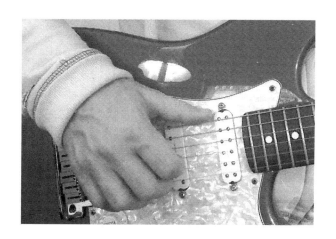

15. Travis Picking

Merle Travis was an excellent finger picker. He was famous for being able to play a bass line with his thumb while he played a melody with his other fingers at the same time. The result was something that made one guitar sound like two. In this song you to play two chords with the Travis picking pattern. The pattern for your right hand is 6th string thumb, 3rd string pointer finger, 4th string thumb, and 2nd string middle finger.

Tips
Doc Watson, who was an excellent finger picker said that it took him ten years to get good at Travis picking.

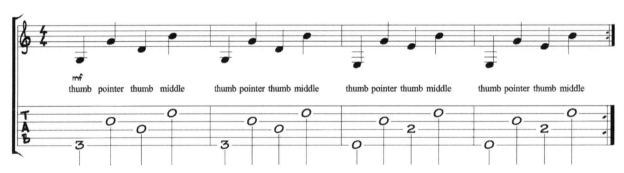

16. ALOHA

Hawaiian music is a happy-go-lucky style of music that will bring a smile to your face. The instruments that create the famous Hawaiian sound are the ukulele and the lap steel guitar. Hawaiian music was popular in the 1930's, 40's and 50's. Today the same classic sounds are being recreated in cartoons like Sponge Bob Square Pants. This song will teach you the Hawaiian style. In order to play the chords in this song you need to barre across the 1st, 2nd and 3rd strings with your pointer finger.

Tips
The chords below are called major 6 chords. Major 6 chords are characteristic of the "Hawaiian" sound.

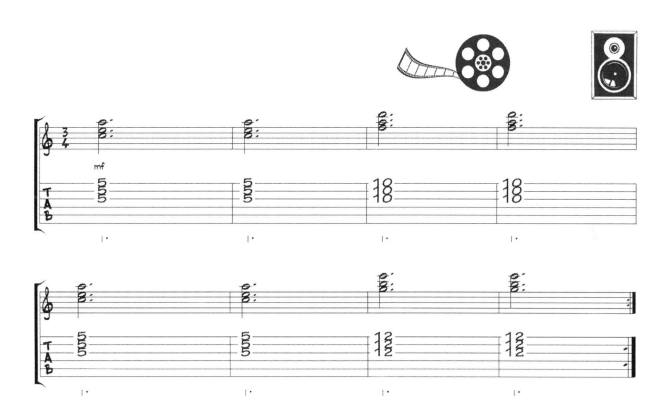

17. MY FIRST BALLAO

My First Ballad is a slow song that will teach you two new chords, a new version of G major and Cadd9. When you look at the chords written in the tablature they appear very complicated because of how the notes are stacked vertically. If you don't like reading the chords from the tablature then use the chord diagrams above each measure to see where your fingers go. Strum each chord for times and then repeat.

Tips
Keep your ring finger and pinky on the notes of the 1st and 2nd string for the entire song.

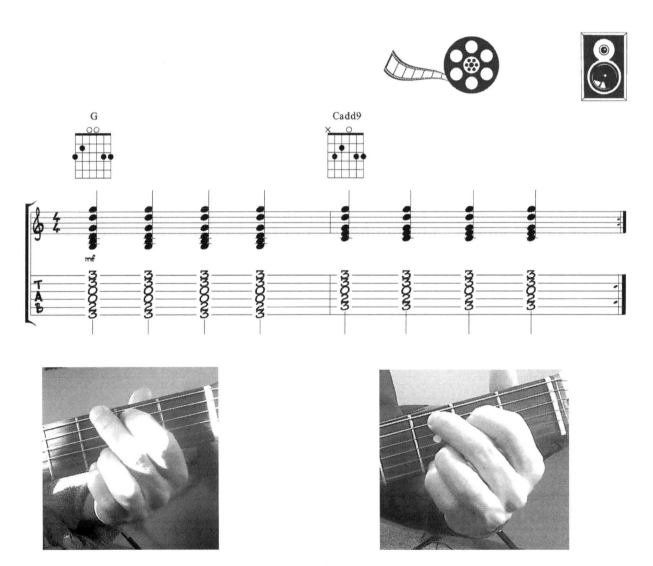

17

18. CATCHY ROCK SONG

This is a fun riff that is made up of two parts, A and B. Play the A part four times, then play the B part four times. After you have played both parts return back to the beginning and play the entire song again. Practice using different fingers of your fretting hand.

Tips

If you are already pretty good with your pointer finger or middle finger, try playing with your ring finger and pinky. Eventually you want to be good with using all the fingers on your fretting hand.

19. MY SECOND BALLAO

If you can play the four chords in this song then you can play many other songs as well. Many famous songwriters use these chords to write music. Strum each chord four times. Please refer to the chord diagrams above the tablature to figure out where to place each finger. You can keep your ring and pinky fingers down for the entire song since they are used to play the same notes in every chord.

Tips
Mix up the order of the chords to make your own song. Try experimenting with different rhythms and strumming patterns.

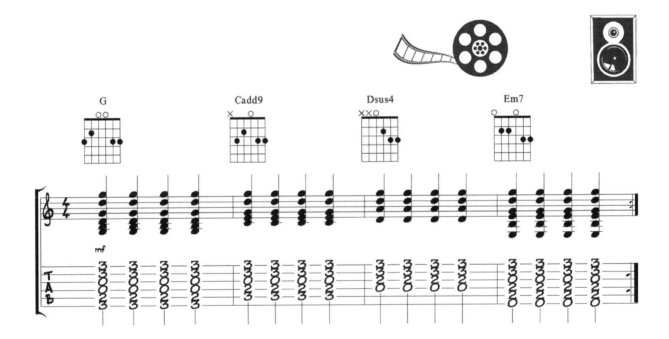

20. CHINESE FIRE DRILL

This Asian inspired riff has been used countless times in movies, songs and television shows. To play the song barre across the 1st and 2nd string with your 1st finger. All the notes in this song will be played on the 1st and 2nd strings and they are all barre chords.

Tips

Remember that barring is when you use one finger to hold down several strings at the same time. If you barre with your pointer finger then put the pressure of the strings on the thumb side of your finger where it is bony instead of on the pad of the finger.

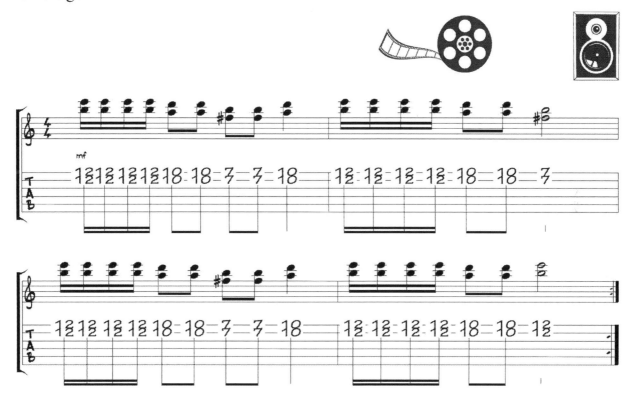

21. FUNKY STRUM

Funky Strum is a song made up of two chords, D major and E minor 7. D major is a very common chord that all guitar players should know how to play. Switching between chords is the hardest part about playing songs with chords. Luckily, the switching between chords in this song is basic. Once you get your fingers in the correct place playing it shouldn't be too difficult. For both chords avoid strumming the 6th and 5th strings. Keep your 3rd finger planted on the third fret 2nd string for the entire song.

Tips
Don't despair if your chord transitions are slow. It can take up to a year to change between chords without a break in between them.

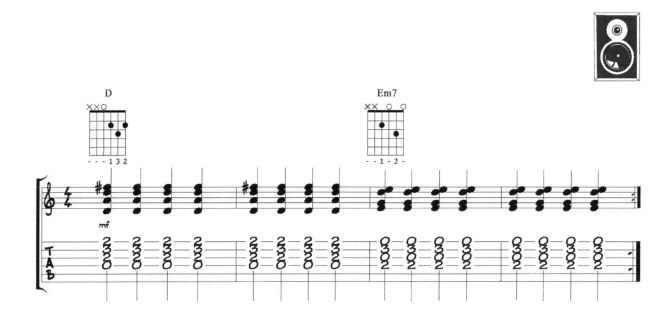

22. THE BLUES

Don't be scared by all the notes! This song looks long and there are many notes but that doesn't mean that it's harder than the previous songs. This song is based on the music style of the blues, which is basically a twelve measure song that repeats. The first four measures of this song is a repeating riff on the 6th string. After that you play the same riff two times but on the 5th string. Now, return to the 6th string and play the same riff two more times. You will then play the seventh fret 6th string eight times and then the fifth fret 6th string eight times. Following that is the first riff, which is played one more time on the 6th string. In the very last measure you willplay something that is called the "turn around."

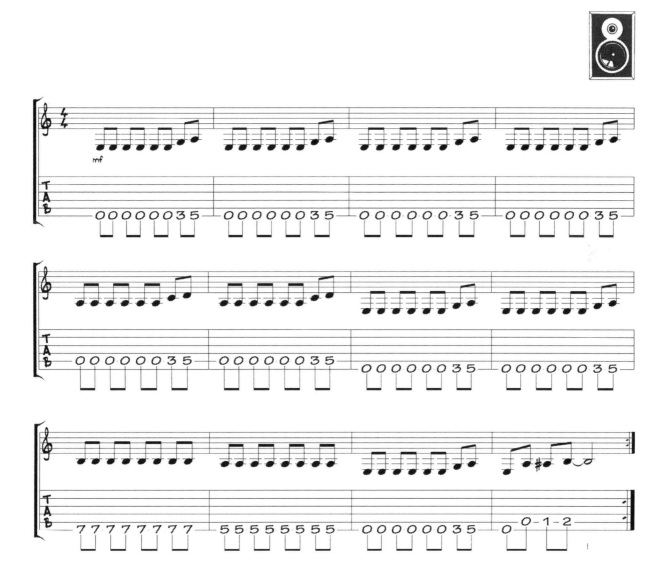

23. MOVIE SOUNDTRACK

This song is reminiscent of a movie sound track. You will be strumming three chords which are D major, Dsus4 and Dsus2. Start by putting your fingers on D major. The rhythm that is strummed is counted 1-2-3-and-4. To play the next chord, Dsus4, add your pinky to the third fret 1st string. Then return to D major. Then play the next chord Dsus2 by removing your middle finger from the 1st string second fret. Watch the video for more details about the strumming rhythm.

Tips
The "sus" in Dsus4 and Dsus2 means suspension.

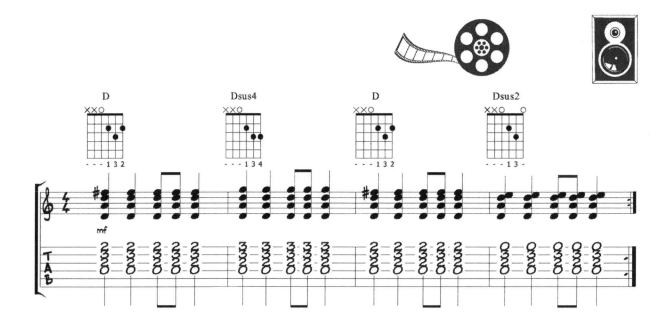

24. BLUE ROCK

Blue Rock is a song based on alternative rock music. It features the power chords that were used in "Powerful Chords." This time you will play different voicings of the same chords. To play the first chord A5 put your 1st finger on the fifth fret 6th string. While holding that note down place your ring or pinky finger on the seventh fret 5th string. Hold both strings down and strum the 6th and 5th strings together. The other two chords D5 and E5 are pretty much played in the same manner, but just in different locations. D5 is the same as the first chord A5 but it's on the 5th and 4th strings. The chord E5 is played on the seventh fret 5th string and ninth fret 4th string. Play with a steady, driving rhythm

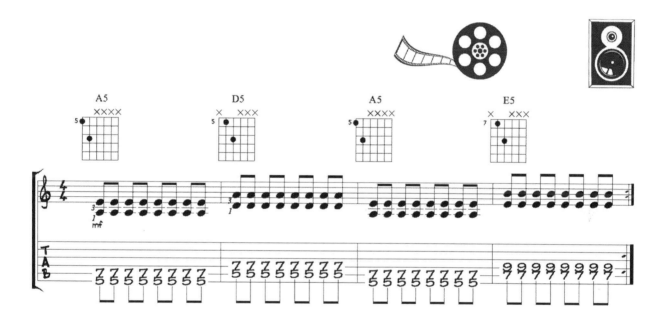

Tips

Use your pinky if you can't reach the notes with your ring finger. If you are unable to play power chords then simply play the bottom note of each chord to simplify the song.

25. HEAVY BASS

The final song is this book is "Heavy Bass." It is a song that gets its inspiration from the band Led Zeppelin. It is based on a one measure repeating riff. This riff is first played on the 6th string and then played on the 5th string. In the ninth and tenth measures you will play power chords. In the last measure there is a diagonal line between the notes 5 to 12. This means that when you play the fifth fret note you will then slide your finger up to the twelfth fret. If you slide while keeping pressure down on the string then you won't actually have to pick the string again to sound the twelfth fret note.

Tips
If this song is difficult for you then practice it in sections or by line.

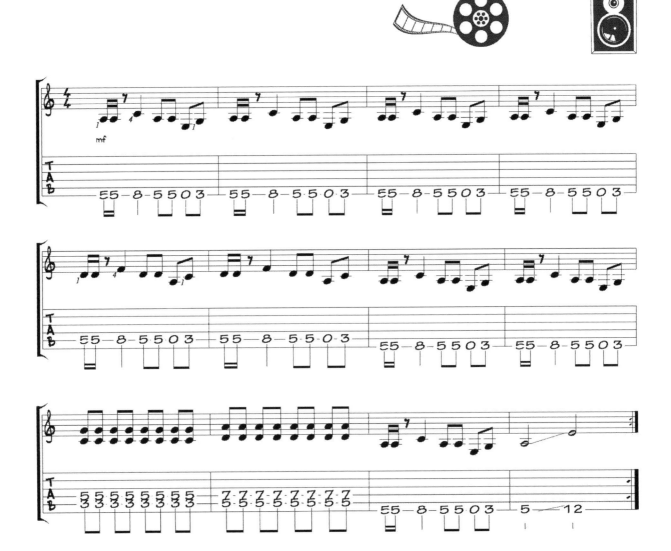

25

NOW WHAT?

Congratulations! You have played through all 25 songs. You should now have a good idea of how to jam along to music recordings on the guitar. This book introduced picking, strumming, and finger picking. There are many guitar techniques were not introduced in this book such as: hammerons, pulloffs, slides, string bending, and advanced strumming. These advanced techniques will make your playing sound more interesting as well as allow you to play more complex songs. These techniques will be addressed in the next part of this guitar series. Thank you for purchasing this book and taking the time to learn to play the guitar. Music can be a very rewarding experience.

THANK YOU!

YOU CAN FIND MORE INFORMATION ABOUT KELLY WEEKS' BOOKS AND MUSIC AT
KELLYSMUSICBOOKS.COM

Printed in Great Britain
by Amazon